Your Soul

Awakens

the Sunset

Françoise Hélène

Your Soul Awakens the Sunset
Copyright © 2022 by Françoise Hélène.
All rights reserved.
No part of this book may be reproduced in any form
without written permission from the author.

www.francoisehelene.com
Endless Books Publishing

ISBN:
978-1-7399500-3-3 (paperback),
978-1-7399500-2-6 (ebook).

Your Soul

Awakens

the Sunset

Françoise Hélène

It's what I do best:
go deep into the roots
and open the wounds.

*My soul cannot help but write
about immortality.
Hence, the foundation of its being.*

Contents

Images of the Soul	1
Childhood Healing	6
The Awakening	32
Words of Advice	58
An Understanding Between Souls	84
Love Notes	112
A Letter to You	125
The Book	130

Images of the Soul

The Foundation

The soul is pure.
Free of social status,
work label,
identifications,
unattached to possessions
and the tangible that vanishes
from the eyes with time.

The soul, sheltered by the body,
transcended by looks.
The invisible is seen
through the actions of the heart,
and a heart is meant to love
and so, it is meant to ache.

The Creation

The colour is evergreen,
and ever-changing.
The touch delicate and fine,
it is made of tulle and silk.
Which do you prefer,
neither or another?

There is no design.
Add what you'd like.
There is no gender too,
choose one that fits you.

Darling, what do you need?
A rope, scissors, tissue?
Shape your soul raw and bare.
Carry it over your skin.
Don't let society carry it for you.

Craft every part of your personality,
create who you want to be.
Embrace every dimension of you.
Because if you choose to be someone
other than yourself,
how will you breathe beneath
the layers of their skin?
How will you exist
in a life that isn't your own?

Who Are You?

When you're alone, who are you?
Will you tell me if you're still the same
and wear your school or work uniform at home too?

Do the thoughts you've learnt from others
still affect you?
Do you still smile as much
as when you meet someone new?

Do you inspire yourself when you feel low
and post on social media like influencers do?

So will you tell me when you're alone,
who are you?
Or would you rather keep yourself
to yourself and hide the truth?

Childhood Healing

Françoise Hélène

The Seed

How
can a seed grow
if it's oblivious to the reasons
it was created:

To fall into earthly darkness
through the warmth of parched soil
and rip from the earth.
To feel the raindrops nurture
the ground-breaking roots.

To rise towards the cheerful light.
Face the world and its deceits –
Hold strength in its stem.

To flourish at its own pace,
among species that grow differently.
To love what it is not,
admire what it is.
Discover the origin
of its existence,
understand the layers
of its composed self.
Own its spirit's presence
in the material world.

Kill its thirst for living
into conscious joy.

Touch the invisible softness
of a mild summer wind
gliding on its skin
from top to bottom
of its entire being.

To adopt a hunger for purpose.
Search for what it needs to thrive.
Accept where it was planted,
learn to be patient and
let its emerald wings sprout open
in returning seasons.

To smell the unusual fragrance of its beauty
and embody its essence.
Empower the visibility of the heart.
Let its petals unwind,
unfold the colours of its soul
to the world and for itself.

To prevent from diminishing
into numbness,
a premature soul-death.

It is its duty, after all,
to evolve and transform
into something greater than itself.

A Star on Earth

You've not known a heart like mine before.
It is made of stardust
and shaped like a full moon,
rotating inside my body
to find its place.

It sees the world differently
and wears the eyes of constellations.
I live as they do.
Here on earth,
I feel non-terrestrial.
Small and suppressed,
in the nature of my intensity.
Too quiet and too loud.
Too hidden and too seen.
And I cannot find space
to rest in-between.

My historical presence, framed
between the walls of my skin,
wonders if there's a loss
to human existence.

My thoughts, misunderstood,
travelling from the air
that my words need to speak
to a celestial language that sometimes
make me feel weak.

I long for my being
to fill emptiness
in a universe
which I have lost
where it is.

Starseed Born

Thousands of years into the journey,
your soul-light,
ancient as daylight,
seeded by stars
etched inside of you,
rises in the cage of your ribs.

A flame shoots to the heart.
Do not extinguish it,
not even with tears of grief.
Let rain and sun pour
through days, through storms.
Feel sentiments suffused
with rawness
inside your bones.

Burn every self-doubt.
And find the power within
you to be who you are,
and enlighten the world.

Reincarnation

You live differently when you're dead:
A friend, a wedding ring, family, your body;
hatched into dust.

Love, enclosed in the grave
of your open heart,
fragile in memory, like the moments
you collapsed crying, into a beloved's arms.

The world lured itself to you.
A rebirth vision unglued your eyelids.
Allow yourself to see life
as an evergreen playground.
Water the roots, let yourself grow,
absorb the minutes with passion,
feel them dissolve in the changeless past
through the ticking sound of a longcase clock.

The older the years, the quicker time passes,
the more frightening silence gets,
as beat by beat, the heart
exhausts its breath.
Then history builds itself again
and creates another bridge for you to cross.
One stone after another,
you learn to reinvent,
you learn to surrender.

Firstborn

A couple's smiles linger in a hospital room,
a moment yet to become a cherished photograph.
A baby's cry awakens its breaths,
heartbeats' whispers are now seen
and lie raw on the chest.

A bed is found in a mother's arms.
A small hand wraps around her thumb –
devotion, touched.

Meanings of life sink in the blood
of the parents' hearts.
Life begins anew and is now for three.

Three kitchen chairs.
Three plates on the table.
Three spaces on the sofa.
Three times more joy.
Three times more sorrow.
Three times more learning.

And no less than three times more love.

What is a Home?

What is a home, you might ask?
The answer is not concrete.
But I must tell you what it feels like
to have a home.

It's a feeling
of familiarity, warmth, and unconditional love
as if you had been separated
by a coma, from a person
who was holding your heart
and coming home
after years of abandoned hopes.

It is a feeling of homecoming
when crossing an ocean
to reunite with your family.
It's stillness like peace after years of war.

It's a soul merging to become whole,
accepting and cherishing the body.
A loving mind, detaching from the ego.

It's being home
after being homesick for lifetimes.

The Foundling

Like a foundling,
I never thought home was a place.

A home is like a starry sky
that wraps itself around the ceiling of the night
to hold you in the darkness
but cannot be touched.

A home is like a heart giving
fearless love, wide as the space
between the earth and the sky.

It's the warmth of a shelter that brings comfort
like the reassurance of a night
returning after a day.

It is dreams yearning for you
to believe you'll be okay.

A home is like a moon
that cares for the stars,
without them begging
for their light to stay.

Children's Dreams

Morning comes and children rise in the world.

Outside, the wind blows strong as if muted
tornados have slept on the hills for the night.

We've woken to their hollow presence
and fleeting fears.
Musical, spasms of summer drifts,
the elevated sound
of blackbirds' songs,
forbidding us to stop dancing.

Guiding our footsteps
in a timeless venture. Restless,
we change ourselves to kites,
pale as the blue sky,
chasing dreams on the mythical hills,
as the grassy path grows
a thousand years longer.

Meet Society

I remember I once wore shoes
the size of my grown-up hands.

As a child, I saw life
infinite in imagination.
Limitless, possible
is how I perceived the world.

People around me
expressed their support for my dreams
through articulated enthusiasm.
Back then, envy was almost non-existent,
faded like a blur of a memory from a distant past.

My beliefs that made the world a better place
had zero boundaries.
I used to climb confidence
on imaginary mountains
that sometimes turned into trees.
Through my heart I depicted
movements of people's personality –
their status, accomplishments or money
was of little importance.

It was easier to love
without the consciousness
of worldly matters.

It was acceptable then
to display the heart's function
in public. Pieces of my wounded heart
spilled across the park
when I'd get a scratch on my knee.

These were the days of our raw selves,
unworried about judgement.

Sunsets pass and we see the world.

Exposed and influenced
by invisible clouds of dust
in consumed air.
We come to understand life:
culture, society, school, government, politics, media.

The more you hear and see,
the less you imagine
and the more imprisoned your thoughts.

My sorrows now
tucked in the pocket of my eyes
under sleepless nights.

My heart captured,
caged in flames, torn into ashes.
The residue, the smoke
filling sickness inside of me.

Françoise Hélène

The soreness, delaying the blood
from circulating, profoundly
aggravating the wounds.

Day after day, the world keeps asking
how I am feeling, encouraging
me to respond with a bruised smile,
as if a heart could beat in stillness.

How can I breathe clean air like this?
How can I be
non-polluted with thoughts?

How can I free myself
when what is expected of me
is to restrict a truth that causes my tears
to bleed in lamentation,
suffocate as the pain deteriorates
within my veins
a little more with every
word or action
that lies.

Ornaments

The evening lasted years.

Your mother loved designing
original pieces of art
but you seldom looked at them.

She had gone
to the yearly fashion show that night;
I was there to teach you,
keep you safe,
stand by you.
I remember you, carrying
a heart that wasn't yours.

In the afternoon sun,
you had sat beside your mother's strength
for hours to watch her sew the blood-coloured patches,
the needle gently dancing between her delicate fingers,
stitching the overheated wounds
between her past and present.

It was you and not the washed-out light
illuminating the pathway
of the night to the closet's door.
It pulled you in like you had fallen into a hole,
the earth vanishing from you.
You found yourself in another world,

aching to belong.
You had lost yourself
in this obscure place,
hiding under your mother's
oversized clothes,
her long, silky burgundy dress
gliding on your body
like a doubtful child sliding down
a water slide for the first time.

For a moment, you held your mother's soul,
her pains embedded in you,
alongside her joys,
which seem to come slower
as one gets older.

Wearing her golden necklace
with an Aquarius sign,
your mother's personality pressed
to the middle of your chest,
dissolving into your being.

You were no longer yourself
beneath the layers,
the material, the skin, the flesh,
the fear of self-identity.
Distant from yourself,
gasping for air,
eager to feel the rhythms
of your heart again.

Yielding its strings
to find a cure for the dullness within.

I had taught your mother
and so, your mother had taught you,
you must wear your own soul.

You are the art
and you are too beautiful
to pretend to be someone other
than yourself.

Françoise Hélène

Weighted Scars

I like the playground when it's empty
but there I play no games.

I sit on the pavement, gently fold my knees
against my chest and pull the spear
out of my heart to let tears flow.

Alone, I breathe like the darkness
at the bottom of an ocean.

School years are heavy.

The weight carries hurricanes
into my bones. Eager
to rip the joints
as thunder strengthens
beneath my silence,
I scream for help.

A hurtful word breaks me into pieces,
like a single strike of lightning destroys a tree.

Here, I am drowning. Can anybody hear me,
or have my tears become
wandering waves of poetry?

The Yellow of Golden Chain Trees

I saw a film in my mother's eyes
on my pre-school graduation day. My life
sped to scenes of adulthood.

My body decorated in a navy suit,
a tie for best manners,
Sunday best shoes,
and a certificate encouraging worth.
Things unfitted with time.

My soul, afflicted among cloned children
on the prestigious stage. I made my way
to the other piece of my heart, my mother,
pouring tears over herself
like a waterfall.

I thought her reflection
could have shown her
the beauty of her being,
but the light was blinding.

My arms locked around her neck,
tight as a necklace,
I held her heart and felt it
breaking in my infant hands.
The deformed pieces
moulding the saddest smile on her face.

Françoise Hélène

Mother had once told me,
as we passed by golden chain trees,
to not be fooled by only what we can see.

I was five and held the vision of a child.
While I looked at the world with a curious mind,
after years of living she understood
adulthood seldom resembles childhood.

Rapid memories rush in her mind;
in a distant decade, she was present.
She was an eight-year-old child when her mother had died
and hadn't felt child-like joy since.

Parts of herself buried within her,
floating in stillness.

In her heart, there was love,
the kind which can only exist with grief.

Her pain, accumulating like a snowball,
dripping in my half-closed palms.
With the heart of a child, I loved her
when hurt unintentionally melted
the make-up on her on cheeks
and equally, when her eyes glowed
with happiness, her laugh,
echoing endearing music in my ears –
The love I have for her is safe and free.

Years later I still remember the moment,
when her tenderness kissed
my left ear and she whispered,
almost as it was long-life advice,
'You sweet darling, carry your wings
and fly. And certainly, oh certainly,
carve your own path. As you grow,
your playful charm is yours to keep.
Most of us spend time playing in our childhood
and spend the rest of our lives
forgetting to do so.
And that my dear is as mortal
as the beauty of golden chain trees.'

Inner Child

Time elapses in the past.

The house is empty, I think.
There is no light in the lingering corridor.
Memories fall into darkness.
My eyes ache to fold.
My footsteps run.

There's an open door
through which you can see a bedroom,
decorated with the happiest of yellow.

A four-year-old child is sitting on the bed.
Her body, fenced between
the daffodil walls.
I wonder if she's a painting of my imagination
but the up-and-down movements of her chest
tell me she is breathing.

I wonder if she knows she's alive
or if she is fooled by the complexity of her mirage.
She cries and the sharp sound of pain
is a soprano melody –
How lovely to set an imprisoned sadness free.

I wonder if she realises I came to listen.
Her tears, screaming to be heard.

I wish to give her my voice
so the world perceives she exists.
Though she must feel her presence herself.

I want to tell her what I've learnt,
not from what the world claims to know
but from what I taught myself throughout the years.
I tell her to keep her soul
when the world will ask her to give it away.
I tell her she's beautiful and I'm proud of her
and I never stopped loving her.
Even when I couldn't tell her,
even when I hadn't shown her.
All along, I have loved her.

Sweet four-year-old child,
childhood years can never be changed
but you as a person won't always be the same.

Let your ear sleep on my chest,
feel the rhythm of my heart
and know I'm here.

She gives me a touch
of much-needed warmth and survival.
Her agony rests in silence on the tissue of my bones.
This time, I allow myself to weep
and I become the music.

She looks at me with mirrors in her eyes –
thirty ages travel by.

I tell her I must go
so I can continue to grow.

I kiss her forehead, abandon her past.

I get up and close the door, locking
our conversation within her facades.

She breaks
the glass window wide open.
The gateway is now there
for her to escape
that childhood home
that used to be mine
in that weary life.

The Awakening

There comes a time when the soul awakens to its most authentic essence. This process is called a spiritual awakening, where one sheds layers that no longer align with the soul. These pieces become distant or lost, then to be replaced with what fulfils one's soul's uniqueness, purposes and growth.

A spiritual awakening is often caused by major life changes which are followed by fleeting bliss, the dark night of the soul or a low state of mind, and a need to search and find a deeper sense of belonging, purpose and meaning on earth.

The process is highly emotional, and the soul transforms, moulding itself into its truest being. When the soul awakens, one realises the power of authenticity in oneself.

Awakened

A new life calls in the middle of the night.
You answer and let go of control.
Respond how you wish.

'Come to me,'
said the self who dies
of false identity.
'You must live nobody else's life,'
said the truer self.
'Feel the flesh of your existence
between your skin and bones,'
said the body.
'Embody your being,
and be whole,'
said the awakened soul.

Chaos

With gripping hands around my hips,
I hold myself.
I fumble and collapse
on the spiral staircase
while the clock in my eyes stands still.
My life spills
to pieces.

The growing emptiness is dreadful:
the temporary job, outgrown friendships and
untrue parts of myself; revoked
as if there is a house inside of me
and my organs tremble
without the support of its body –
belongings lose their home
and the home loses its belongings.

Lost in my compass,
I learn to sculpt the way.
Revive the dead needles,
encourage them to depart again.

Leave the broken with reasons
as my heart opens
a part of my mind
I did not know existed.

Fleeting Bliss

This morning,
humanity interlaces hands
around the earth,
like zodiac signs
in a natal chart.

Curtains of sun expand
in my house and the distinct scent
of freshly cut grass settles
in a place I have never known.

Gothic gates open into a garden.
I inhale the air, transparent of taint
and it grasps the freshness of a
mild spring day, slowly
ageing in warmth,
dissolving into my blood.

The news, absent
of content. Their silence, golden
as a shooting star's footprints in the night.

Wars, extinct in futuristic vision.
People, embracing existence,
serving love to living beings;
intertwined, connected,
united by the pulse of an angel's heart.

Françoise Hélène

The world rejoiced.
Rivers and oceans sailing
sunny auras across continents.

Sadness uncreates itself –
constantly melts in the yolk of the sun.

Loneliness buried in graves,
separating touch from death.

People are wanted pieces of art –
decorations of the world that please the eyes,
blossoming like flowers without thorns.

Lands, thriving in the weather.
Communal libraries, well preserved
since the seventeenth century.

A daughter forgives her father
for the years of unfilled emotions he gave her.
An ex-couple become friends after a divorce,
relationships fix themselves in the family.

The wealthy use their spare bills
to help the ones with no homes,
no employment, and
anyone who can't afford therapy.
The CEO of a corporate company
offers coffee to the receptionist.

The man with fuchsia hair receives
compliments from strangers on the street –
tenderness is willing, easy and free.

But this is
an illusion
of the past,
present
and future.

All is
avoidance.

All is
a dream
in which I sleep
for a world like this
to appear ever so real.

Françoise Hélène

Post-Bliss

I do not intend to change the world
but I certainly intend to inspire change.
So, some of us can heal
the beaten patches of human endeavours.

The Dark Night of the Soul

The darkness slowly pierces
your skin with its knife.

An immortal presence
within you ruptures
a blurry, evergreen path
where you learn to walk
towards your raw self –
meet yourself, like a child
recognises its reflection
in a mirror for the first time.

Seek the light and you will see
light in the journey.
It is not the sun nor the moon lighting the way,
it is the light of your soul.

Françoise Hélène

The Sky Pours

Moonlight hours are extended by days.
At home, the sky mourns
and pours to the window,
and through, my iris darkened.

The land overfloods in my eyes;
a crow has mistaken my reflection
for its nest in which
lie shadows of thoughts.

My torrential loneliness is nocturnal,
the love of the night howls
as it understands my grief,
meets me in softening cries,
kisses the depths of my despair,
and embraces the bleakness of my scars.

Sorrow Flows

Inside the body, the heart holds tears
like a river of blood
yearning to perch in its vessels
like a coffin resting in a grave.

The current seizes me away.
As my hand slips
from a rock,
the tides conceal me
under the water and draw me
to a place of terror.

I'm overflooded with palpitations,
attentive to their anxious music;
with higher consciousness
each movement strains my muscles.

My throat tightens,
my lungs shrink to the size of a pea.
Air enters me in fragments.
I strive to tear my heart,
to immobilise emotions,
as they pierce flesh
through my chest.

Vicious thoughts rage
in my mind and my heartbeats drop.

Françoise Hélène

My breathing loudens
and inhales grief,
like a lost child crying out
for their missing mother.

My soul is restless.
Alive, fearful
of an afterlife.

The air is weeping,
impressions of death floating on the day.

Perhaps it's only natural for one to suffocate
in a contained environment.

We cannot live without sentiments –
instruments of life.
With little music also comes little life.

So let your sorrows flow
across all bodies of water,
including your own –
and the current shall pass.

Temporary Solitude Bliss

I have been there, where the heart slowly dies
in concrete silence that shatters brick walls.

It's a place I feel unloved
but I am still whole.
There, the light is lost,
even the stars are full of sorrow
and have turned dark.

The cold wind invites my bones to shiver
and my smile frowns into a cry.
The wounds open, tears
gently stain my skin.

Streams of anguish flow through me.
I am the artist of sorrow and the paint dries
like depths of the heart speak
a foreign language to the shallowness
of the eyes and end connection
 between souls.

Solitude is comforting,
blissful,
salvation.

Questioning the Meaning of Life

The earth had been bigger than usual.

Seas of constellations
bathed in the starry sky.
I could choose how to travel,
along with my possessions.
I carried my soul
and looked at myself as if I'd forgotten
who I was.

Without knowing where the paths
would lead,
the day of my birth
I began searching
for meaning.

In my mother's arms
there was a relationship building;
the essence of affection that grows
when you are held
next to a beating heart.
But this period soon passed.
In my teenage years
there was love in the movies
and I had learnt from romance novels.

I was a character of life itself,
nothing like the novels,
nothing like the movies,
except the ones I'd write
individual characters for.

Growing into adulthood,
people talked about self-love.
Apparently, it was something no one could give
me, no other person than myself.
I liked the ideology, at that point
in my life, I thought it must exist.
So, I kept searching,
not for love, but for meaning.

I had spent years scrutinising
world maps, researching content
of continents, travelling with faith
across countries, cities, hidden villages,
unnamed places, beyond the map.
From mountains, hills and valleys
to oceans, lakes, rivers, sinking boats and shores.
I was the sand, hauled by the sea,
ripped under the sun, longing
for transformation,
as if it was possible to become
a raindrop and find home in a cloud,
see the world from a bird's-eye view;
outside of myself.

I kept exploring in unusual places.
Year after year, the meaning was the same —
unfound.

Until the rebirth of a beginning arrived
and I had thought twice,
where is the meaning?
And I had thought once,
what am I seeking meaning for?
And I did not know the answer.

The Last Sunset

On calm evenings when the sun parts
with the light of day like this,
after our absences had missed one another,
fifteen years ago,
we met four times a week
and sat on the quiet hillside
overlooking the city,
famous for its river and towers.

In front of the blood-orange sunset
we'd sit on the pale, silky vintage picnic quilt
knitted in magnolias, and eat our favourite foods:
strawberries, olives, cheese and crackers.

Conversations merged sealed secrets
between trust and promises, yet to keep,
if retained in memory.
You held my heart as it was yours,
and with two hearts come
double exultations, twice as many sufferings.
When you smiled, I was there to support you;
when you cried, I was there to hold your tears.

We met in an unspoken place
of receptive understanding.
With you, I could be myself
without overthinking my words and actions.

With open arms, I was adored and accepted.

But time taught me
not everything we treasure
stays forever.

In sweet melancholy,
a story at last ceased growing;
like darkness grows upon sunsets,
some chapters slowly fade as journeys do.

Moments change and our heart
feels less of the same.
I have learnt to love
is sometimes to let go,
to set free
and love again;
other times
not wanting any more.

Dear shared memories are
sometimes best loved by history.

In untold goodbyes, for the least, I knew,
by parting mutually we'd both grow.

Though when you see a sunset again,
I hope you'll remember me.

Déjà Vues

I was no longer young, standing
on that fatigued ground where I
had been, before this skeleton was formed.

Oblivious, I was pressing on my grave.
The roses, unborn into potpourri
over the scent of damp mud.

A heart cut apart from mine,
with its feelings still beating in my chest.

I had other lives, the proof
engraved on a stone between
the story of a first and last name.

The soul escapes the digested body,
and past fears emerge
through dry growing weeds.

The coldness of regrets touching
my dead skin,
I had been good, trying to heal
my forgotten sins.

Which residues of my soul
were living or dying,
I no longer knew.

Françoise Hélène

But what I knew is that I
was no longer young,
standing on that ground.

My soul born old,
feeling weighted
and weary from past damage.

Emerging Soul

A day in January,
the coldest in years.

The night is kind,
uncertain and deep.
Midnight trees,
far away set the obscure scene.
The blackened sky yearns to be seen
yet all that is left to do is to feel
its presence
as its heaviness falls.

The wintry air pierces
a touch of discomfort
through my flesh,
turning it into ice.

Seeking warmth
my thoughts pause,
the world disappears,
my breath softens my skin.

My soul
now visible.

Seeing the World in a New Light

All I have loved,
I loved with all my heart,
and changing the way I love
erupted an ache
worth dying for.

A New Path Begins

We must see the dark to know the light
just as we must feel sorrow to know joy.

The soul sleeps in the night for years
beneath blankets of frost.
Time is frozen and waits
to show you sight of day.

Awake.

See the darkness fade
into the clouds and look at them move
between shades of blue.

They too wander uncertain journeys
towards unknown endings.

Words of Advice

Between Walls

The wooden door is heavy as I pull it towards my heart.

Unfamiliar with the place, I dissolve
into the counterfeit walls.
Strangers laugh, as life itself is a comedy.
Tears aren't welcome here, neither is grief.

To smile is to be beautiful,
even if meaningless, even if numb.
That is how you drain yourself
into emptiness.

But I've learnt to be less cruel to my needs.
So, the truth is lying on my face.
It hurts to stand alone
in this mirage of overwhelming happiness
and futile noise:
the business, the rushed traffic of humans.
It is a myth to think
a heart that cries does not belong to laughter.

Melancholy demands a shelter
where it can happily be
with and without sorrow.
It is a place that invites both,
I find rest and room to grow.

Françoise Hélène

Allow Yourself Time to Weep

The sound of sorrow isn't meant to remind us
of a weakened heart
when all of us carry such natural music.

A heart beats with survival in all humankind
and we are brave enough to overcome a pain
strong as if death was twisting your throat.

At times, all that's needed is to pause,
allow ourselves to fall,
live in our thoughts,
meet with sadness, sit with its mood,
become its companion
and stay for the night in cold sentiments
to find strength
in the story of ourselves
we share with the ones who hear us break
into silent tears
and understand the call of our growing hurt
from the shattered notes
of our vulnerable melody.

While they hold our music,
we must write new lyrics.

In Times of Sorrow

Unstitch your sorrows
from your nerves.
Twist your torso
like a drenched cloudy cloth
that's fallen from a boat
sailing across oceans of rain.
Be hopeful the waves will take you
to a dry, sunny island
that's forever lost.

Detach from the shallow earth.
Dive into the water.
Touch the carpet of sand.
Breathe.
Don't let yourself drown.
Drain the ink from your tears.
Draw a stained melancholic smile.
Pour your feelings into poems.
Envelop them in a ghost-coloured bottle
with a tragic melody
and send yourself to sea.

Perhaps in times of sorrow,
turn yourself to nature, art, music or poetry,
anything that opens the hurt
in your body to dissect the pain
to set it free.

Seek a Friend

When your heart is sick of loneliness,
make time for a friend and stay away from your enemies.

Gaze at the sunset and feel the love it brings for the night;
inviting the moon to shine its brightest –
see the light, ally of the darkness.

Be with a friend who cherishes the depths of who you are –
secrets will be told and so will be kept.

In good company, shorter are the days.
And if a love is true and present, longer it will stay.

Stay and you will see,
the more the years pass,
the more meaningful the friendship becomes.

So, seek a friend who guides you towards the light.
Seek a friend who cares enough to listen and to speak.
Seek a friend who gives attention to your existence.
And be a friend in return.

Find a Supportive Environment

Deprive the plants of soil, water and light,
and even if you love them,
none can grow.

Capture the sea, in your kitchen sink,
and see it flood the floors.
Stop the earth from moving,
watch the sun turn into shadows
of eternal night.

Cage your soul in normality,
feel it become dispirited.

Elect leaders of inequality,
meet a world of protests.

Anything in the wrong environment
remains a prisoner of others
and oneself.

Think for Yourself

The classroom has no walls:
teachers are all around us.
In buildings, houses, parks, sidewalks,
they fill environments with messages
that become subtle knowledge.

Everywhere you go,
detect the distant noises
breaking through the echo
and the voices murmuring through
the price tags at the supermarket, the lyrics in music,
the colours in your phone's application,
the scent of food at restaurants,
and the screens you open to the eyes of the mind.

This is how the world tells you its secrets;
question why they are told.

Notice thoughts of the day and thoughts of the night.
Reflect on what you read,
what you see,
how you feel and look
within
to understand.

Choose Your Own Path

On this new morning, you must go.
Take your heart,
soul and mind, too,
and forget me
for as long as you need.

Step into the mist.
Follow a path.
Choose the scenery.
No one can find you,
you must find yourself.
In the unknown and turbulence,
uncover what makes you feel at home.
Be kind to yourself.
Resist fear but listen to its voice.

Move towards the north,
but if your heart leads you south,
go there instead.
Question your actions
and see answers reveal themselves.

You can lose track of time,
but don't lose sight of the importance of the days.

And whether we'll meet at a destination,
I cannot tell if the voice of our silences

Françoise Hélène

will choose the same heart direction
nor if the distance will grow
into love or abandonment.

The Artist

Be the artist of your life.
Create your own beauty
and let it be yours to love
with fearless passion.

Françoise Hélène

Connect to Your Intuition

Sit somewhere calm
and close your eyes.
Quieten your thoughts,
hear the absence of noise.
Listen to the molecule of air –
notice the sound of you.
Feel the blood travel in your veins.
Rest your hands on your heart,
feel the rhythm of each heartbeat.
Find peace in your instinct.
Let it pull your skin
like a magnet in your stomach.
Bathe in the beauty of your silence,
explore the entities of your soul
and admit the guidance of your being.

Shed Inauthentic Layers

You must exhaust your fear of being known
to allow your truest self to exist.

Open the Wounds

Do not dread discovering your soul.
Touch its roots,
split the aged wounds,
let the blood weep.
Acknowledge the hurt,
carve the origin of its flesh.
Feel the heaviness suppressing
the middle of your chest.
Press on the open pain –
release its breath
and let yourself heal.

Find What Makes You Feel Alive

Happiness is found
in a lot of places within the soul
and finding them is well worth
our time.

Learn

Sufferings open the eyes
of precious knowledge of the heart,
which is learnt by surrendering the pain.
And to surrender is to learn
to mend the soreness.

Connect with Nature

Sunset has come early and it feels like home.
It wraps me in its arms without permission
and in the sweetest of beauty
my soul chooses to linger.

Its warmth and safety engulf me
in its deep orange gleam.
I keep its wisdom,
which grew year by year
before arriving here.

'Always stay hopeful'
whispers the sunset
as its peaceful colours absorb
into my obscure, sorrowful heart.

To Give Oneself Time

It was winter all year round,
and I went to lie on my bed after the earth
removed the sunlight.
Eyes wide open, perhaps, I couldn't sleep.
Contained in the darkness,
it had become my environment.

My friends resented meeting me there,
afraid it could illuminate and bring clarity
to the darkest parts of their beings.
For this reason, solitude is sometimes my life's
companion as its old calmness accepts me.

We both choose to stay in stillness
as long as it's nurturing.
Our mutual love complements
our harmonious moods.

Soul over soul, hearts intertwined,
solidarity lives in me.
We hold hands and I do not let go,
as I cannot leave
a part of myself behind.

Embody Your Life Purpose

Some mornings, I wake alongside the sun.
Even when invisible, I know it's in the universe
and I dedicate my presence to the day.

I sit in the garden and admire the changing
apple trees throughout the seasons,
helping my soul age in wisdom.
The open air liberates me –
the world lives in me.
The hours are minutes.
Passion is prosperous
and at no cost,
more than free.
So, I write my heart's desires
on linen rag paper,
across blended stains of coffee spills.
Words drip off my lips.
Thoughts ink blank pages,
which now teach me about society,
various knowledge
and thousands of philosophies.

They share unheard voices,
build a sense of community,
show support in epiphany,
and help us understand humanity,
no matter our identity.

Françoise Hélène

This is why I love writing poetry.

And you, what would you do,
if the day would last a lifetime
and the tiredness of the night would never arrive?

Choose What Matters

When time knocks at your door to choose a path,
choose what matters most.
Your soul in accepting environments.
Your voice in reciprocal conversations.
Your values in intended actions.
Your companions in your soul's missions.
Your heart in your life's decisions.
Your mind in your future's ambitions.

In One's Life

Seek passion, be passionate
and passion will surround you.

Allow yourself to love what some may not,
show love around you and love will find you.

Take time to understand yourself and others,
and a world of clarity will grow within you.

Share your universe with the ones who value you,
have life teach you,
and see yourself guide others too.

Seek Truth

Be authentic to who you are and seek truth.
This is how what you need finds its way to you.

Seek Knowledge

To gain knowledge
is to nourish the soul.
Though, must you gain knowledge,
do not strengthen the ego,
for then, all nutriments shall be lost.

When Stars Align

When you feel lost
or misunderstood,
wait for the night
and look at the stars.

They too have waited
to shine lights of hope
to help you guide the way.

An Understanding Between Souls

Eyes of the Heart

Lasting beauty is more than skin deep
and listens beyond the introduction of the body.
It is seeing growth after challenges
and the story behind a smile.
The embrace of joy after sorrow.
The entity of the soul.

Hence, a beauty that cannot be stolen
by progressing tomorrows
is seldom seen
but felt and understood
by one's heart.

Françoise Hélène

A Love for Deep Conversations

The mountains sat quietly,
listening to the crickets' murmuration
in the yellow grass.
The clouds suffered from the heaviness
carried by droplets of tears –
the ambience turned grey.
In the heart of the silence,
two voices walked there.
One was of the ocean,
the other of the shore.

You dreaded the darkened mood
more than the silence.
The transparent earth,
holding the homeless stars.
You stood on the shallowest hill –
a world emerged in the soil between us.
Our souls rose like barriers between
winter and summer.
Your cheeks blushed,
red as the coldest of stars,
you saw the dark for once,
at last,
you thought.

Words, spinning in my mind,
a dream-like land.

I wished for the knowledge of the galaxy.

I wondered if heavenly bodies
were trapped in the sky,
felt alive, worn out or were eager to die.
I wondered if a universe lived in them too
and if, like me, they urged finding the reasons of existence.

Beneath their white glow,
I questioned their presence,
alongside mine.
While you gazed at me with puppy eyes
as if I was no longer human,
had taken the depths of the nightfall
and had become the darkness itself.

Françoise Hélène

A Love for Reflection

Calm and peaceful is the soft
tinkling sound of raindrops
touching glass sheets of wind.

Clouds of thoughts come slowly
from the blurriness of the heart.
For the light to exist
some days must be dark.

Today, the world lost its soul
and searches for itself around me.

Restless shadows of hopes travel
on the other side of my window –
I see two of myself:
a vision where the mind is free
to wander in abstract reflections,
the other, restrained.

Compassionate Heart

You've got pretty green eyes.
You remind me of my nephew,
when he was two.
But grief was missing
from his arms. And I never learnt
to deal with it.

Seeing you lie on the hospital bed,
death quivering over you.
It is too soon to separate
my existence from yours.
I need more years
to love you, hold you,
sing you lullabies before sleep,
offer you cuddles in the mornings.
Now, I can only sit next to you.
Your fragile breath
touching my skin at intervals
like a sudden flush of winter wind.

You are brave, holding
strength for both of us.
Every time you speak,
the softness of your voice
stitches a new heart into me.
I want to give you a new life,
one with a cure,

and take away your haunted sufferings
before they take you.
I want to give you my smile
in exchange for your tears.
I see through you,
you're beautiful –
you hear my thoughts,
your soul whispers,
'I'm growing towards the light
and so you are.'

Heart Keeper

A dead smile
in a stranger's eyes.
I meet another's tears,
they now belong to me.

They show me their scars,
the wounds bleed in my hands.
Their pain, important as my own.

Fear of death enters me,
fear of life is there too.
I am immortal
and the hurt swells inside of me.
My heart beats faster and accumulates dust.
Its gateway torn apart,
darkness arrives
and builds a home.

Memories that aren't my own
engraved in the flesh of my skin –
each remembrance
dissolving into scars.

Françoise Hélène

Immortality

Between the walls of this medieval cathedral,
I enter the lives of dead strangers.

Precipitations of lifelong griefs,
bottled-up sentiments in the clear air.
Here, no feelings are dismissed
and we can see their saturated hues.

The soul is the skin of the body
and results in my heart's ability
to envision emotions excessively
through a gaze of detailed observations.

The smoke from the dying candles
gravitates across the transept
and through a white mist.
I cross over to another world.
Paralysed in a dream –
I am chained in a dungeon
of souls, transparent in body.

My skin rips like cotton sheets,
as I separate from them –
their absence
fulfilling years
of emptiness
into my heart.

Afterlife

It's been four decades since our souls fell in love.
Now, we still sit in the shade
in the wooden copper chairs
on the porch of the house we bought
when we had slight wrinkles on our skin.

The navy lake, surrounded by trees offering
a Constable painting's view.
There, we often read in silence, your hand
touching mine between your favourite pages.

We're like poetry –
engulfed in sweet hours of conversations
to keep our minds sane.

I had learnt to love you
day by day. Our lifetime,
brief in this way.

I didn't want to think about our funerals,
I didn't know which would come first.
But if I could I would ask to keep you with me
for as long as could be,
for our breath and our health
to live in synchronicity,
for our love to be preserved
at a celestial museum.

Françoise Hélène

Change the cycles of what we've learnt
about the universe to a newborn theory.
So you and I can meet after death
and question everything we believed
when we were alive.

A Love for the Past

My heart is fond of ancient things
that carry history in their vintage shells.
I am the earth awakening the rising sun
and fall asleep to the clock of the moon.

I write letters on my typewriter until the light
of burning cinnamon candles melts the world
around me into complete darkness past midnight tea
to let the ink bleed into the darkened world.

I draw with charcoal on rocks and pavements
until my wrist cannot bear the tiredness
and screams to rest to begin again.

I take black and white photographs of human shadows
to remember not the beauty
but the secretive depths of a person's darkness.

I bathe outside in the pouring rain,
the cold of each drop kisses my skin,
I absorb its scent
like a body perfume.

I spend Saturday mornings in antique shops
and get gems I don't need.
Even when I promised myself I wouldn't buy anything.
I wrap each item in my arms like a parent holds

their newborn child
to bring the touch of their delicate skin home.

I lift the emotional weight of the person who worked
centuries to carve fine details in carefully curated items.
I collect rare objects from spirits
and feel the rawness of their sentiments
in extended dead hours of life.

I gently wipe the dust off records
and sing along with Beatles songs.
I travel to ancient libraries
to smell old books and decode the meaning
of floriography as if I was living in history today.

I cherish the words of departed writers
and fall for wisdom, truth and chivalry.
I drag their bookish, immortal bodies
to their graves to help them heal the grief
of lifetimes' stories.
I meet with souls I haven't seen in a century or three.
We catch up in quiet parks with deep
conversations and organic coffee.

Because I, I yearn for unexplainable familiarity.
My soul cannot help but search
for items, places and returning old friends
resembling, more or less,
what they did in previous lifetimes.

A Quiet Day at Home

Quietly the morning sun rises
and liberates the hours ahead.
Time hides in a wooden, antique treasure box
and flees out of sight.

The kettle puts itself on,
tranquillity is home
and it's comforting to know it's here.

One floor up, the living room is restful.
I rise on the stairs, with the garden view,
water the peace lily and sit in the forest
green velvet chair.

A thousand year old book rests in my hands
until a page sleeps in my dreams,
then my quill wakes under the low-lit stars,
my mind is understood again.

In the kitchen, hunger calls,
life slows down.
My fingers spread a glaze of honey
on the winter-baked mood;
the heart is now sweeter.
Late-evening tea awaits in the bathtub,
soft amethyst waves smell of lavender
and envelop the calmness of a sea around my skin.

Candlelight changes the atmosphere to sundown
and next to this kind of world
I lie between the solace of cream satin sheets,
and in its power to comfort,
I immerse myself in the fallen night
and awake to the relentless rain.

Unmaterialistic

When the sun opens its radiance to the west
side of our country home,
pineapple-shaped crystal glass
on the narrow shelves varnishes
the white kitchen walls into golden wealth.

Their reflections evaporate from time to time,
like a broken heart arrives without warning.
Their shine fading into dullness –
a heart of stone.

But if you pay attention to the oil painting
facing the arched window,
you'll see the glasses unfilled,
incapable of sentiments,
vanish into pennies.

Open the window alongside a page of history;
a love story from the late eighteenth century.
Green leaves attached to oak trees,
grown blackberry bushes, bright flowers in the garden,
the mild summer breeze caressing your hair.

A man wears a long, brown waistcoat
with the confidence of his mid-thirties.
He's walking towards you,
his hands serving as a basket
to hold fresh vegetables and the scent of wet earth.

He was a farmer at fifteen and cultivated abundant nature.

The woman is beautiful too. Hazel eyes, engraved
with compassion, wearing a cherry linen
dress with elegance, her silky
light blond hair balancing on her shoulders.
She gazes at the stars
when the sky hasn't darkened
and has forbidden them to glow.
Like them, the couple show care
through silence and conversations.

They had met in a place of solitude.
They were alike; nonconformist, eccentric,
living in a past era,
while the world lived in modern times.
Their hearts had fallen in love before needing affection.
Companionship unfolded slowly,
like a lost letter in the post.
It took years before a first date at the park.
Their home gravitated towards plants, gardens,
rivers, paintings, antique books, soft melodies
and her writing poetry.

She often collected flowers in the meadow,
the alive and the dead ones,
turning some into art – she loved them equally.

Most evenings, the neighbourhood could hear
her vocal instrument spreading classical notes

across the residential street
while cooking. He played soft strings to join in,
cleaned the dishes while sheets of mint
brewed in hot water for tea. They liked helping
each other like that,
mutually.

Love was timelessly growing in acceptance.
And on half-empty nights,
the moon was the light in the living room.
He sometimes held her close in tenderness,
feeling her heartbeat against his chest.
Peeling her forest green and black corset off her body,
lingerie left on the spiral wooden staircase.
The tips of his fingers embracing her silhouette,
inviting him to touch her with respect,
naked and bare, essence,
he loved her for more than that –
for the intangible sides of her
that activated his mind and fondness for another.

Three years of love, but no child had come.
Life goes on, though differently.
The relationship germinates emotionally,
seeded connections, willingly imprisoned
through each other's hearts.
A home filled with space
to dance in the evenings,
welcome friends and family.

Françoise Hélène

And there in the painting, the cottage is similar to ours
but in the kitchen, no crystals are to be found,
only pennies,
covered in dust.

Dreamers of the World

My sister and I used to run in the wild field
behind the house. There were no walls.
Some days we'd disappear from the world
among the four-foot ferns, much taller than us.
Our arms high, pushing through paths
like explorers in a cruelty-free jungle.

We held the world in our hands,
our dreams were endless, within reach.
We'd often lie next to purple tiger roses
on a bed of faded teal, dry leaves.
We laughed under the funny-shaped clouds.
Sometimes brought willow flower baskets
yet to fill with unfolded secrets.

I'd told her things I wouldn't tell anyone else:
how other children thought I wasn't pretty
and looked like a boy with my mushroom haircut.
How it made me drown in low self-esteem,
pour my eyeballs beneath the darkness of the nights,
wanting to become invisible in the world.
Almost every morning, she'd tell me I was beautiful
and lovely, so I came to believe it myself.

I was three and she was five.
She was the reason I learnt what it meant
to have a long-life friend
and appreciation for somebody else.

Françoise Hélène

I remember an evening in August,
her head rested on my thighs,
engulfed in thoughts; there were ants
crawling in her stomach, she had said,
as the skin of our fingers interlaced.

The stars had made us wonder
what school was going to be like for her in September.
I knew how listening to stories
made her happy so before bedtime
my imagination would tell her a story.

We'd hold each other's ladder to climb
to the dreams we had
as if we could hold the stars, without danger.
We said if we'd go to the moon,
we'd eat cheese up there.

It caused my heart to beat softly again,
to see her tears transformed
into sparkly eyes and laugher,
as if an old birthday wish had come true
years later and the tooth fairy
had left coins under her pillow.

Moments between us were a kind of love
I never wanted to forget.
Since the day I came into the world,
my sister ever believed in me –
I will always love her.

Hopeless Romantic

Pure love finds the pathway
to patience in a maze of a hundred avenues.
Faithful love commits
to understand another for the rest of its life.
In time it evolves
from a meaningful friendship
to a deeper bond.
True love is unseen,
felt through the heart,
admired by one's soul,
content on its own,
connected emotionally,
blissful when found,
deeply missed in the absence
of a love ever so true.

Françoise Hélène

Simplicity

When I find myself in nature,
my soul is prosperous and content.
Yet I do not possess
any of the seasons;
I hermit in the gloom of winter
and it fills me with owl hours of healing.
The wounds slowly cure themselves to
escape hibernation and become scars.
From their stems, I grow into the floral essence of spring.
Then, the earliest sun unfolds its greatest florescence,
blissfulness veils sweet summer joys.
I am charmed by the comfort of extended,
warm outdoor evenings.
Then comes autumn,
when the worlds inside
and outside of me transform themselves.
Parts of me die,
others appear –
loss offering gains in return.

A Love for Soul Connections

I yearn for soul connections.
If it is there, I stay and love with all that I am.
If it is not,
I take the lessons and abandon.

A Love for Freedom

I have a deep love
for what sets me free.

Anything that unchains me
so I can uncover my bruises without shame
and admit I need to heal the damage.
Anything that encourages me to grow,
without question, I stay.

But these people or things,
I do not choose to love –
It is out of my control
to adore what knits
wings onto my heart,
and lets me equally
fall and fly.

A Love for Personal Space

I haven't stopped loving you.
Even when I was out of your sight
I loved you between the lines of our shared silence,
the loss, the grief across the distance,
the vivid memory of you.
I love you more
than I could ever write in a poem.

Love Notes

Somebody Loves You

When you think no one
in the world can love you,
not even yourself –
Think of the stars
looking over you.
Feel the universe opening
starry doors for you.
Feel the wounds softening their skin.
Close your eyes and think of me,
because I love you just as much
in the light and in the darkness.

Françoise Hélène

To Love a Melancholic Heart

Few can love
a melancholic heart so deeply.
Though I, the shooting star,
have travelled galaxies to find
a loving darkness where I can breathe,
feel alive, burn for love,
and fall for a heart filled with night skies,
craving to hold the light.

The Growing Rose

If only you could see
yourself through my eyes,
you'd see the loveliest of flowers,
innocently blooming in its purest sunlight,
surrendering through the strength of its thorns,
transforming them into needles,
piercing through the layers of your heart,
transitioning the blood into a sweet morning dew.

It's the way you ascend after you fall
that grows sentiments of love
in all I am.

While you search for the light
your brilliance dims my darkness.
You rise and I, in turn, fall –
for you.
And so I am fond of flowers;
I am fond of you more.

Your Soul is Art

Inside of you there is wisdom
filled with lifetimes of knowledge
of heart and mind.
A pure and genuine soul,
a rare and magnificent beauty.
A piece of art in its natural museum.
You're one of a kind,
and better than any antique I could ever find.

Flower Press

Flowers are meant to bloom
after they die.
Their infinite essence
continues to grow
as they decompose themselves
into a new form –
this beautiful, cultivated growth
is worth preserving.

Imperfections

'With relationships come imperfections'
I said as you laid the rawness,
of your heart on our Moroccan living room carpet.

Next to the fireplace, the warmth lit
compassion in candlelit shadows,
reflecting the sound of our thoughts
in the restless evening.

Your sadness, lying on my bruised shoulder,
welcomes the cold to enter our home.
Your eyes dilute as if the world
 had tormented your soul.
You understood less of it
though more of yourself.

See, you must learn to study the music
when silence brings frightful thoughts.
Appreciate the subtle sound of crackling,
as the logs slowly breathe fear
of falling on one another.

Put your glass of wine aside,
let it be full and not empty you
while I caress your awoken pain,
dissect a little of your brain,
as I'd open a weary science book,
analyse complex emotions of your flames.

See, you got to acknowledge every part of yourself,
along with your imperfections.
This is how to be human,
this is how I can love you.

Françoise Hélène

Grateful for You

Our souls travelled for years
before arriving at a place of longing.
That moment, our world intertwined
and I did not recognise your appearance
but your soul, familiar
like an ancient home in which I had lived
from childhood to the end of my days,
life after life.

Our souls have loved each other
for a very long time and I'll always
be grateful for you as I live
in this life and the next.

Reassurance

I have never loved you
for your looks, your profession, your qualifications,
your race or status.

I love you for the way you see the world.
The way you think for yourself.
Your eagerness and ambition.
Your love for learning.
For the way you allow yourself to feel passion.
For being your original self.
For the depths of your soul that makes you
compassionate and kind.

I have never loved you for your first or last name.
And when a soul loves like that,
it falls in love for lifetimes.

In Darkness

You are brave, to sit in the darkness
and fight the cold
of demons' hearts
while your tears drip
on your skin like droplets fall
from the roof of a cave.

Alone and lost,
blind for hope in the underground –
the dead of night will pass
and you'll see the sun again,
just as I have too.

You have the strength
to go through the ghosted hollowness
of your nightmares while they frost
your breath.

Connecting with Oneself

Rays of sun fall asleep.
The earth crumbles into the dusk.
This place of stillness releases my worries
and the darkness is my sanctuary.
The self dissolves
in winding instinct.
The soul is loud.
The night, pierced
by the sound of awakened owls.
Nothing is lost in the viewless light.
I am safe in peaceful, solitary thoughts –
rising with the stars.

Françoise Hélène

A Love's Touch

If a soul is untouched
by true love in one's life,
may it spend the course of its life
falling in love with itself.

And if true love touches
a soul in one's life,
may this soul fall in love
with itself first so it can love
somebody else.

A Letter to You

Throughout your life there are a lot of things you'll feel like giving up, but you shouldn't be one of them. The universe created you so you could craft yourself and I hope you give yourself the freedom to do so.

I want you to be happy, but life is not about constantly being happy because what causes you to grow won't always make you smile. You'll sometimes feel your world shatter in the palms of your hands and it will hurt like hell, it will cut your skin and make it bleed. But please believe that the pain will pass. Find what helps you process the pain and fill your life with it.

With life come challenges, so know you are strong and you will get through the winding roads. But sometimes this means failing, learning and beginning again, and other times it means to move forward, overcome and continue.

You have a heart that lives every emotion that passes through you; you are whole in this planet of billions of people. Be the one and choose yourself.

You do not have to fit in everywhere you go. Undress the false layers of your soul. Grow your truer self and have no shame in who you are. Expand your mind, think for yourself and do not ignore your soul. It is yours to keep for the rest of your life and beyond.

Someday, you'll realise your past does not belong to your present and future and you are not your traumas, your failures or your sadness. You are a being who survives tremendous hurt and that in itself is a victory.

You'll look at yourself in the mirror and you'll smile because, despite the scars you carry, you'll see the beauty that lives inside and outside of you. You'll realise the lies of someone who once told you, 'You are not good enough', 'You should be more like this', 'You are not beautiful'. You'll accept that not everyone will love you but some people will adore your quirks and your uniqueness, so focus on those people and show them you care.

One day, you'll understand what it means to love and be loved with a whole heart. You'll learn that to love this way is to take the time to understand somebody else, uncover what makes them who they are, be grateful for them and make time to unravel what they need and want; and if they do the same in return, the relationship is golden.

Someday, you'll meet someone who will allow you to share your emotions; you'll fall weeping into the comfort of their arms and they will not disguise or judge you. You'll learn to walk alongside their growth and allow yourself to offer support and be astonished by their evolution.

You deserve caring, supportive and kind people around you. People who listen to what you have to say and take time to have conversations with you.

Love is often spoken through actions, and you matter just as much as the children, family, romantic partner and friends you have.

Give compassion to yourself. You will feel this love deep within you. Don't put up a façade for society, and find meaning and purpose in your own way. Whether that's working at the coffee shop around the corner, being an architect, having or adopting children, looking after your family, helping the community, creating paintings, or becoming a poet, a spiritual healer or an inspirational leader. No matter how big, no matter how small, choose what feels the most meaningful to you.

Find your place in the world and find your tribe. Get to know yourself. Stand up for yourself.

One day, you'll forgive your regrets. You'll look back on your life and you'll be proud at learning life lessons from your mistakes. You'll learn how you heal best and feel the wounds vanish into cure.

You'll be proud of how much you've grown and who you are.

You'll reject the disapproval of others. You'll embrace your uniqueness.

Your heart will be seen and your soul will be loved. And if they haven't already, I hope these moments begin now. I hope this book brings you comfort and love, anytime you need it.

So keep it close to you.

With love,
Françoise Hélène

The Book

Each page is frozen in my hands.
In between I hold a life so dear.
Time passes, and the minutes never return.

My old heart
feels the growth of my soul.
I tell dearest family and friends I love them,
knowing it is words of goodbye.
I store fond memories in the corners of my eyes,
hopeful they'll stay.
In them, I see the joys of an imperfect
but meaningful life.

And oh, what a greatest joy
for the soul to be whole,
before the body dies.

Acknowledgements

Thank you, dear reader for reading my work. I appreciate your time and attention and I hope you have enjoyed my words. I'm thankful to share this book with you. I hope you were able to relate to some of the poems.
I hope you've learnt something from my insight and that you can come back to this book anytime you need comfort or clarity.
Thank you to my mother, who has been my number one fan since the beginning, and my supportive family and friends who take the time to read my books and show me enthusiasm through kind words and encouragement.

Thank you to my sister by heart, Christina, for always supporting my writing and believing in me. Thank you for being my human diary and for always being available for me and for listening to my joys and sorrows. Sometimes, I think you know me better than I know myself. I'm grateful to have you in my life, despite oceans of distance between us.

Thank you to everyone who took the time to read this book before it was published. Thank you for letting me be heard and making me feel as though I matter to you.

Thank you to the universe, for making me go through a spiritual awakening at just the right time so I could write this book. I hope this collection is helpful for anyone who's gone through the process or who can relate to any aspect of it.

As you hold my book in your hands,
I'm grateful for you.

From my heart to yours –

Françoise Hélène

About the Author

Françoise Hélène was born in New Brunswick, Canada and lives in England. She's an award-winning poet who's inspired by nature, music, art, holistic health, spirituality and more.

If you have enjoyed reading this book,
please leave a review online.
As a creative professional, reviews are incredibly helpful
and I'm grateful for them.

Connect with me on Instagram, Facebook and YouTube.
I look forward to seeing you there.

Instagram: francoisehelenepoetry
Youtube: francoisehelenepoetry
Facebook: francoisehelenepoetry

www.francoisehelene.com

Until the next book.

Françoise Hélène

www.ingramcontent.com/pod-product-compliance
Lightning Source LLC
Chambersburg PA
CBHW030303100526
44590CB00012B/495